INSPIRED
Photography Offering Encouragement

by Larry E. Crane
© 2023

*Dedicated to my wife Judith for her tireless support
of my photography and her love for the Lord.*

My photography is devoted to capturing and sharing God's glory as seen through His creation. The inspired artwork in this book seeks to offer encouragement through God's word. I sincerely desire that you are reminded of God's presence and the hope He provides.

Larry

Front Cover:
White Pocket
Vermillion Cliffs National Monument
Arizona

Back Cover:
North Rim
Grand Canyon National Park
Arizona

Opposite Page:
The Needles
Canyonlands National Park
Utah

For since the creation of the world God's invisible qualities - His eternal power and divine nature -
have been clearly seen, being understood from what has been made, so that men are without excuse.
Romans 1:20

"HEAVENS DECLARE"
Maui, Hawaii

As the full moon begins to set across the Pacific Ocean, the heavens are filled with stars as if they are singing praise to God for His wonderful creation. We should never forget that we surpass creation's beauty in God's eyes, for He wonderfully made us. Therefore, we too shall declare His glory and proclaim the work of His hands.

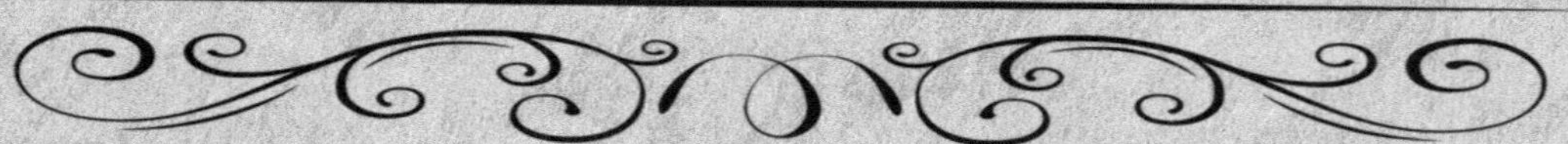

The heavens declare the glory of God;
the skies proclaim the work of His hands.
Psalms 19:1

"BE STILL"
Blackwater National Wildlife Refuge, Maryland

Early morning in the refuge is still but not quiet. Blackwater sits in the middle of the Atlantic Flyway bird migration route and is home to over 700 species of birds. Our lives can be like the refuge, calm on the outside but filled with noise, worldly noise, on the inside. Being patient, as we wait for the Lord, is often one of the hardest things we do.

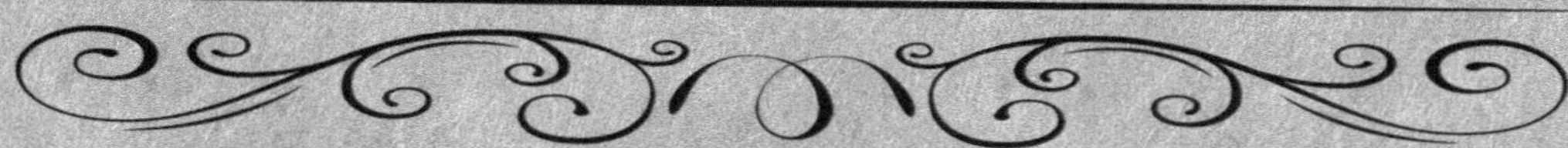

Be still before the Lord
and wait patiently for Him.
1 Peter 3:4

"CUP OVERFLOWS"
Downing Creek Falls, Oregon

It is impossible to stay dry witnessing this amazing waterfall. The mist from the crashing water swirls in a small gorge beneath the falls. This image captures the essence of God's overflowing love for us and its inescapable impact on our Christian lives. We are spiritually blessed beyond our cup's capacity with overflowing grace.

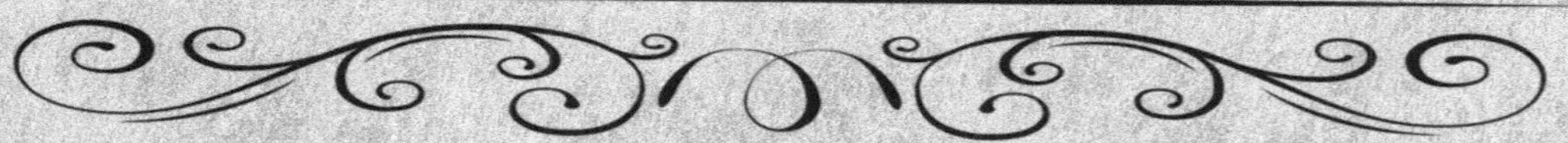

My cup overflows.
Psalms 23:5

"SEARCH ME"
Grand Canyon, South Rim, Arizona

On this very early summer morning, 'God rays' appear to be searching the canyon floor as if God were performing a morning inspection of His creation. God constantly inspects our hearts to see where our true devotion lies. It is easy to become distracted in this overly busy world, and our prayer is for God to open our hearts to Him.

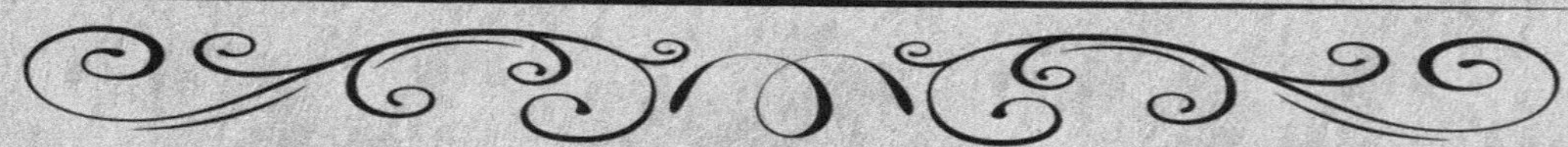

Search me, O God, and know my heart.
Psalms 139:23

"GENTLE SPIRIT"
Mt. Hood National Forest, Oregon

With a light fog on this damp morning, the forest lay quiet, providing a gentle peacefulness. Although a chaotic mess of vegetation, it is beautiful. Likewise, our chaotic, messy lives can be transformed into unfading beauty as we shed the world's focus on outward appearance and focus on our inward beauty that God sees.

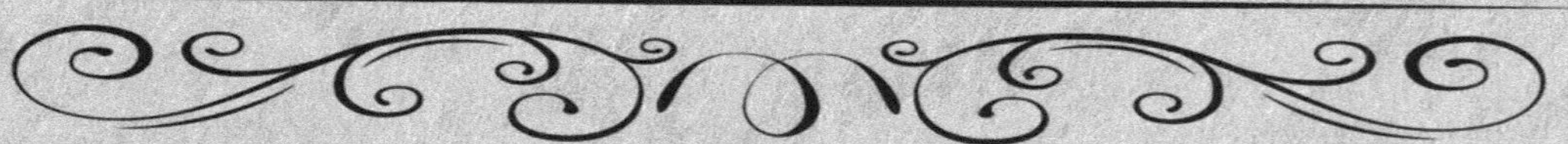

The unfading beauty of a gentle and quiet spirit.
1 Peter 3:4

"RIGHTEOUSNESS"
Mt. Hood, Oregon

Towering above the surrounding landscape, Mt. Hood is Oregon's highest peak at 11,249 feet. Standing majestically against a cloudless sky, it is visible as far as the eye can see.   So does God's righteousness tower above the earth, visible for the entire world to see. His love reaches the heavens while His justice plumbs the great depths.

Your righteousness is like
the mighty mountains.
Psalms 36:6

"TRUTH PROTECTS"
Cape Meares Lighthouse, Oregon

Positioned 200 feet above the Pacific ocean, Cape Meares Lighthouse has protected sailors since 1890 with its distinctive red-and-white flashing light. Just as a lighthouse provides sailors a protective beacon of truth, God's word offers protective truth in this troublesome world. God's word shines brightly, directing our path toward Him.

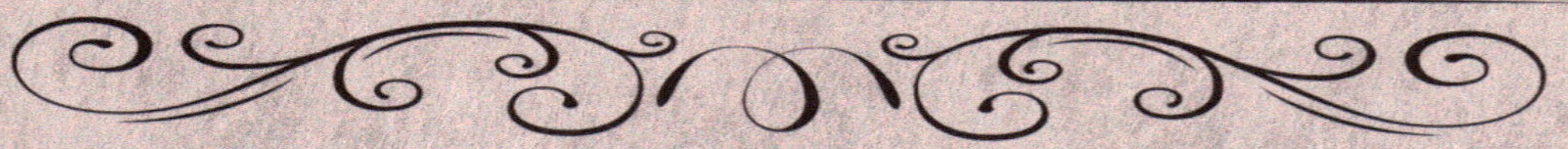

Your truth always protects me.
Psalms 40:11

"BEAUTIFUL"
Glacier National Park, Montana

The magnitude of God's beautiful creation erupts during Fall in Glacier National Park. The mountains radiate permanence while the fall leaves demonstrate fragility. Our Christian lives, while secure forever in God's grace, are fragile with easily broken hearts. But God is good, and His love for us immeasurable.

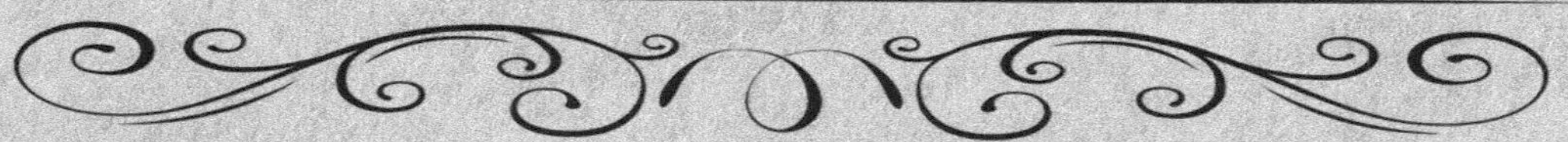

He is good; His love endures forever.
2 Chronicles 7:3

"LIVING WATER"
McKenzie River, Oregon

As the turquoise waters race downstream on this early Fall Day, the melting snow high above in the Cascades provides a seemingly never-ending supply of life-giving water. Through the Holy Spirit, our Christian lives can produce flowing streams of living water that nourish the spiritually thirsty who are around us.

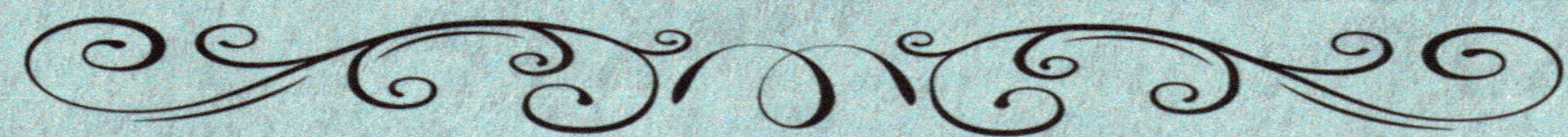

Whoever believes in me, streams of
living water will flow from him.
John 7:38

"PEACE"
Sparks Lake, Oregon

Steam rising from the warm water of Sparks Lake on this brisk morning creates a peaceful setting beneath South Sister, which last erupted 2,000 years ago. The juxtaposition between a threatening volcano and calm waters reflects our lives. We live in a fallen, threatening world, yet God provides us peace "at all times and every way".

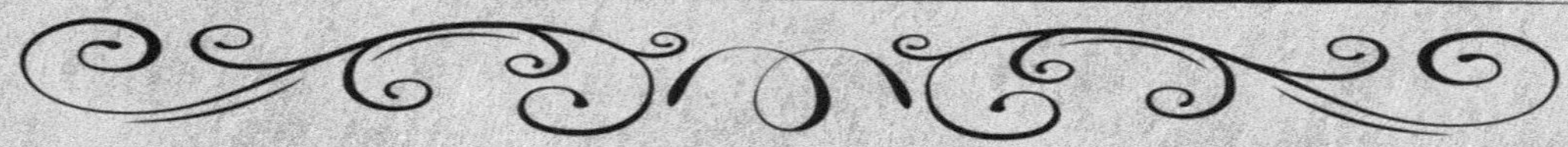

May the Lord give you peace
at all times and in every way.
2 Thessalonians 3:16

"MY ROCK"
Zion National Park, Utah

The Great White Throne rises impressively 2,350 feet above
Zion Canyon's floor. Its sandstone rock shows the wear of time
and the elements. While our lives also show the wear of time and
experiences, our Lord never changes, never showing the wear of
time. He is steadfast in His love for us, delivering us into eternal
salvation.

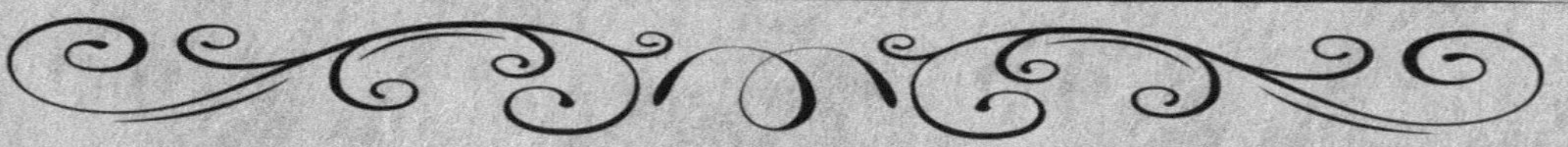

The Lord is my rock,
my fortress, and
my deliverer.
Psalms 18:2

"RESCUE ME"
White Pocket, Vermillion Cliffs, Arizona

White Pocket is an isolated and desolate geological wonder where one marvels at God's creation. Given its remoteness, one feels alone and vulnerable. At times we feel isolated, vulnerable, and in need of spiritual rescue. Yet God is always near, always. Our refuge is in the Lord, as He is our rock, a strong fortress to save us.

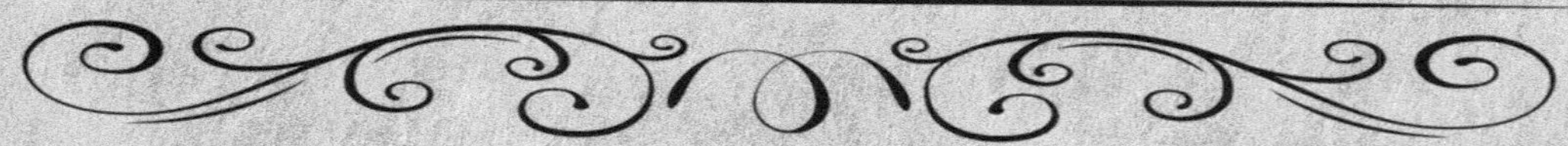

Turn your ear to me, come quickly to my rescue.
Psalms 31:2

"POWER"
Shore Acres State Park, Oregon

Crashing waves can reach over 100 feet high, releasing the enormous power carried by ocean swells generated thousands of miles away. Yet, as incredible a display of the ocean's power, it pales miserably compared to God's power. A mere glance at creation confirms His great power, a power that loves us beyond comprehension.

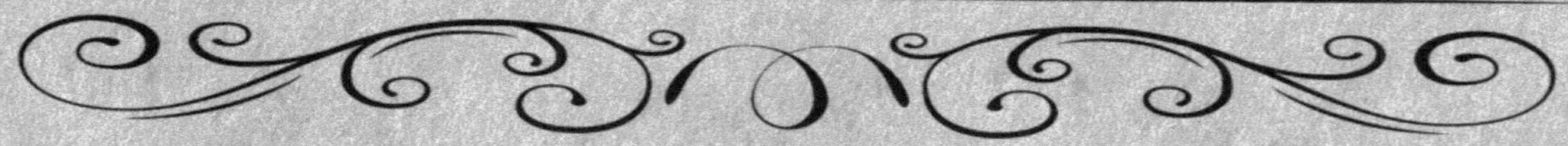

So great is your power.
Psalms 66:3

About the Author

Creating memorable images using photographic techniques is a love affair that traces its origins to my childhood. For me, it is about creating a "Wow!" reaction, about being provoked emotionally by the beauty of God's creation. In today's oversaturated world of mobile device snapshots, I think it is ever more critical to capture the world around us in a meaningful, thoughtful, artistic manner, thereby creating something of lasting value.

My first camera was a hand-me-down Kodak Disc 4000 from my grandparents. Maybe not the most technical camera in which to learn, but it stirred the intrigue of capturing moments in time. After college and starting a family, my go-to camera was a Canon EOS Rebel 2000, which documented our family's life and continued to push me to be more creative with these important images. In 2008, digital photography entered my life with the Nikon D90, then the D7000, then the D600, then I stopped chasing the digital upgrade path to pursue something more: Large format 4x5 film images. With unparalleled image quality and camera control, large-format cameras offered me the greatest creativity and long-term image value available. The limitation is my imagination.

My image collection spans several years across digital and film platforms. Lightroom and Photoshop are just as essential for post-processing as the darkroom was to early photographers. But the most significant value of an image is the combination of the image captured, it's post-processing and the final print.

An image only realizes its full potential when printed. I truly hope you enjoy my work!

See more at https://larrycrane.net/

In Christ,
Larry